Look At You!

A Book About How Your Body Works

By Kathleen N. Daly
Illustrated by Kathy Allert

*Prepared with the cooperation of
Bernice Berk, Ph.D., of the
Bank Street College of Education;
and William B. Gurfield, M.D.*

A GOLDEN BOOK • NEW YORK
Western Publishing Company, Inc.   Racine, Wisconsin 53404

Note to Parents

As young children grow, they develop their own personalities and a sense of who they are. Just as important for children is an understanding of *what* they are—their physical selves. This book gives an informative and enjoyable introduction to the human body, and parents will find it helpful in presenting the subject to their children.

Many of the body's functions go on beneath the skin, where children can't see them. But children can begin to understand how their bodies work when things are explained in concrete terms. You can remove some of the "mystery" surrounding the body and help to prevent misconceptions by laying a clear foundation for your child. Wherever possible, help your child to relate the text to his or her own body and experiences. For example, you might ask your child to make a muscle or do a stretching exercise, as suggested in the book. Or you might want to discuss the section on digestion with your child. Start by talking about familiar parts of the body, such as the mouth, teeth, and tongue. Then tell your child what they do. Finally, explain that eating and digesting food enable people to grow. Once your child understands this, he or she will begin to see the importance of eating nutritious foods. After all, the body is like a machine, and it needs the proper fuel to run.

Of course, a book of this size can provide only simple information and perhaps a springboard for more questions and answers between you and your child. Encourage such discussions, for your child's curiosity about his or her body is both healthy and natural.

—The Editors

When a baby is born it is small and helpless. It can't sit up or stand by itself. It can't walk or talk. (But it can cry!) And it has to be fed and cleaned by its mother, father, or some other person.

You were a baby once. But look at all the things you have learned to do!

You can walk, run, hop, and jump. Perhaps you can skate, swim, turn somersaults and cartwheels, and ride a bike. You can talk and think, draw and paint. You can feed and dress yourself, and go to the bathroom by yourself.

You have learned a lot, and your bones and muscles have grown bigger and stronger than they were.

There are many bones inside your body—206 of them! The bones form a sturdy framework inside you called a skeleton. Your skeleton is strong, but it isn't stiff and heavy like the framework of a building. You can move around almost any way you want because you have joints and muscles.

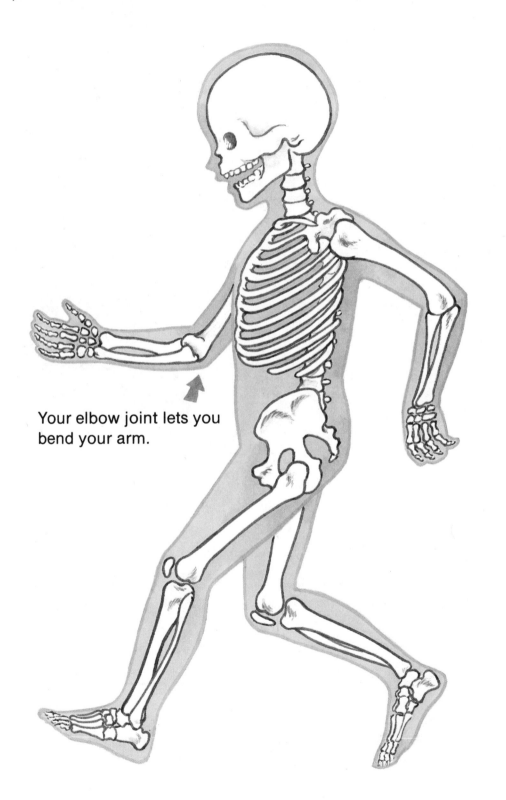

Your elbow joint lets you bend your arm.

A joint is a place where two or more bones come together. The bones are connected but they can move freely, a little like the way a door can move on its hinges.

You can throw a ball because you can move your shoulders, elbows, wrists, and fingers.

You can kick a ball, and run and jump, because of your hip joints, your knees, and your ankles and toes.

Muscles are attached to bones. Muscles are the movers
of the body. You can see some of your muscles at work.

You can decide whether or not to use certain muscles.
You can decide to walk or bend or swing your arms. You
can decide to use your face muscles to smile or frown.

But there are many muscles that work all by them-
selves. They are the muscles that help you to breathe,
blink your eyes, sneeze, digest food, and do lots of
other things that you don't have to think about.

To help bones and muscles grow, you must eat and digest food.

What happens to food when you eat it? It takes a long journey! The journey starts in the mouth, where your teeth grind and chew, and your tongue helps shape the food to make it easy to swallow.

In the stomach the food is broken up still more, so that it can go into the bloodstream and bring strength to every part of the body.

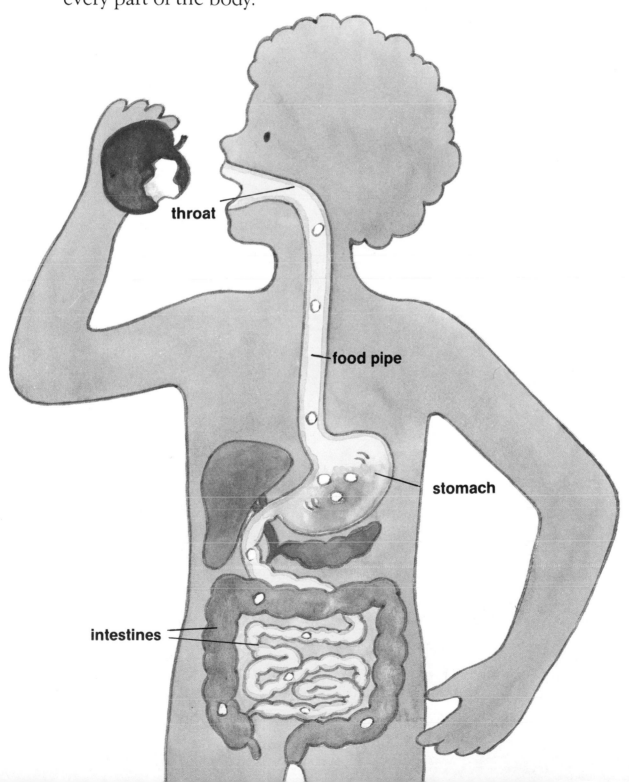

throat

food pipe

stomach

intestines

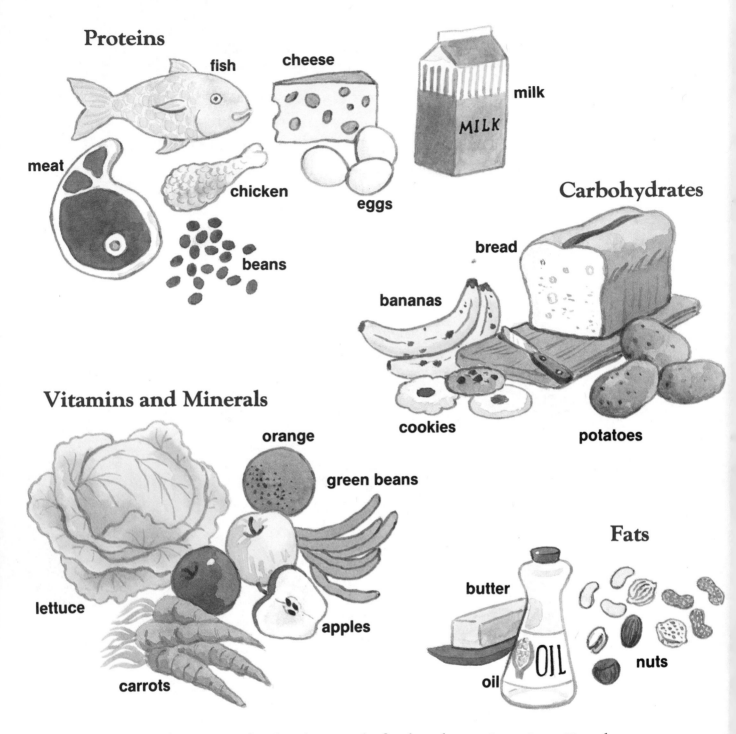

Proteins

fish

cheese

milk

meat

chicken

eggs

beans

Carbohydrates

bread

bananas

cookies

potatoes

Vitamins and Minerals

orange

green beans

lettuce

apples

carrots

Fats

butter

oil

nuts

Like a car, the body needs fuel to keep it going. Food is the body's fuel.

Meat, eggs, fish, and beans help to build strong muscles.

Fruits and vegetables keep your cheeks rosy.

Milk and cheese help to build strong bones and teeth.

Bread, spaghetti, and cereal give you lots of energy.

You need many different kinds of food to keep your body healthy and strong.

Another way to take care of your body is to keep yourself clean. It's important that you brush your teeth after meals and wash every day.

And you can help to keep your muscles and bones strong by exercising. Exercising also keeps your heart and lungs working strongly.

In the middle of your chest you can feel the thump of a muscle called the heart. (It is about the size of your fist.) The heart pumps blood through the body. Blood carries nourishment to every part of you.

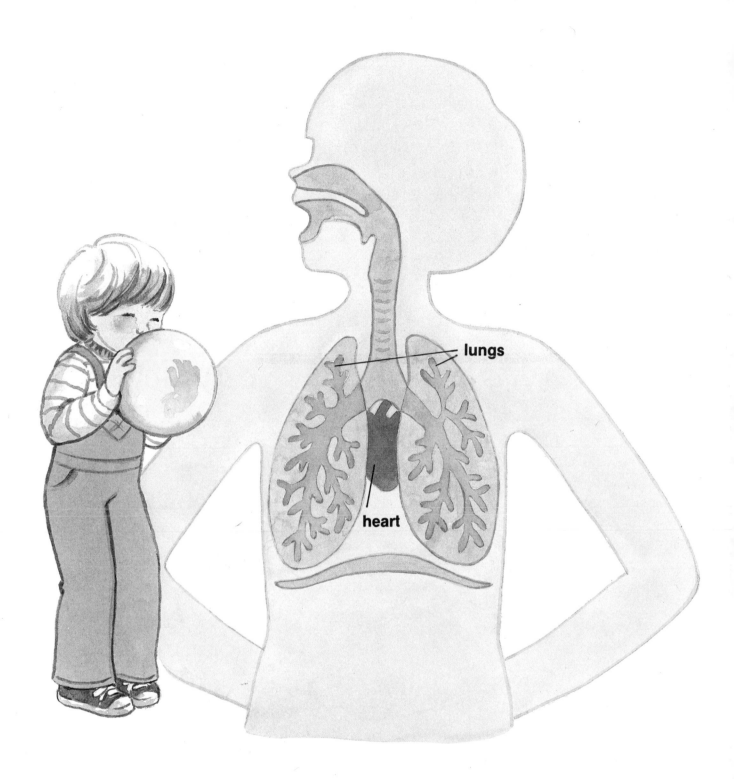

You breathe air in and out through your nose and lungs. The lungs are on either side of the heart. When you breathe in, each lung fills with air, just as a balloon does when you blow into it. Then the oxygen in the air goes into the bloodstream and reaches every part of your body.

What you breathe out through your nose and mouth is used-up air.

Sometimes your body does funny things with air. When you cough or sneeze, air comes out in a rush and helps you to get rid of dust and germs. You may open your mouth wide in a yawn if you are sleepy. Sometimes you may hiccup, and air goes in with noisy little sounds. Or air may come out with a burp.

Other sounds that come from the body as you breathe
in and out are talking, whistling, and humming. You can
feel air moving in your voice box if you put a finger at
the middle of your neck as you talk.

The different shapes you make with your lips, tongue,
and teeth help to make different sounds. Look in a
mirror as you say the letters of the alphabet. You'll see
how your lips and tongue and teeth help to change the
sounds you make.

What are your favorite sounds? The *boom* of a drum, the *honk* of a horn, the *meow* of a cat, the *whoosh* of the wind in the trees?

You hear sounds with your ears. Waves of sound move into your ears and press against the sensitive skin and tiny bones inside your ears.

You see with your eyes. There are many wonderful
things to see.

Look at your favorite toys and your favorite people!

Look at the sky and the clouds!

Look at beautiful pictures!

Eyelashes, eyebrows, and eyelids help to protect the
eyes from dust and glare. Tears bathe your eyes every
time you blink, and keep the eyes moist and clean.

You enjoy the sight of food before you put it into your mouth. But once the food is in your mouth, your tongue tastes it and tells you if the food is sweet or sour, bitter or salty.

The radish is bitter.

The pretzel is salty.

The candy is sweet.

The lemon is sour.

The thorn is sharp.

The petal is smooth.

The grill is hot. Don't touch!

Kitty's fur is soft.

The ice cube is cold.

The pebble is hard.

You can feel hot and cold things, sharp and smooth things, soft and hard things with your skin, especially the skin of your fingertips.

All of your body is wrapped in smooth, snug, waterproof skin. Skin helps to keep your body at just the right temperature—neither too hot nor too cold. Sweat comes out of the skin through tiny holes called pores. As the sweat dries, your body feels cooler.

If you get a cut that is not too deep, new skin quickly grows to repair the cut.

The color of skin may be pink or yellowish or brown or black. If you stay out in the sun, your skin may get freckled or turn darker. Or you may get a painful sunburn, if you are not careful.

Skin is covered with hairs so tiny that you cannot see all of them. But you can see the hair on your head, and on the faces of men who grow beards and mustaches.

Hair may be straight or wavy or curly. Its color may be white, yellow, reddish, brown, or black.

It doesn't hurt to have a haircut because hair has no feeling. And hair keeps on growing every day.

What is it that keeps your body working smoothly all day and night, even when you are asleep?

It is your brain.

The brain stays alert all the time, getting messages and sending messages to muscles, eyes and nose, fingers and toes, and every other part of the body.

With your brain, you can think, you can remember,
you can decide what to do or not to do.

He is planning his birthday party.

She remembers her telephone
number and calls home.

She decides to stand
upside down.

He decides not to cross the street.

Even when you sleep, part of your brain stays awake. You dream, and in your dreams the brain helps you to sort out everything that has happened to you during your busy day.

And sometimes, in your dreams, you may remember that time, long ago, when you were a tiny, helpless baby. And look at you now!